CW01310306

Copyright © 20123 by YASMINE DAVEY All rights reserved.
This book or any portion of it may not be reproduced or used in any manner whatsoever
without the express written permission of the publisher
except for the use of brief quotations in a book review.
First Printing, 2023 ISBN **9798857078020**

Oceana

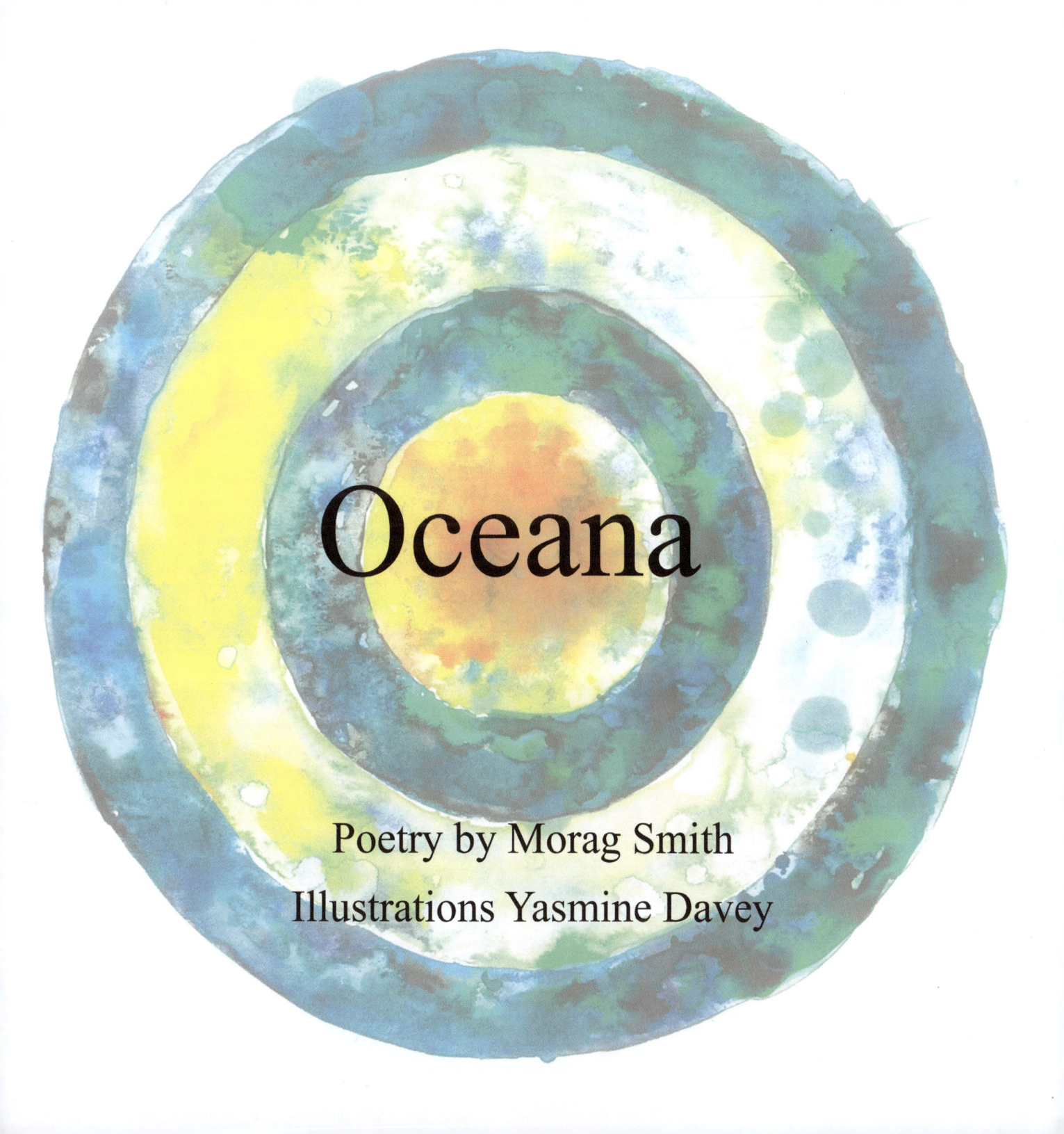

Poetry by Morag Smith
Illustrations Yasmine Davey

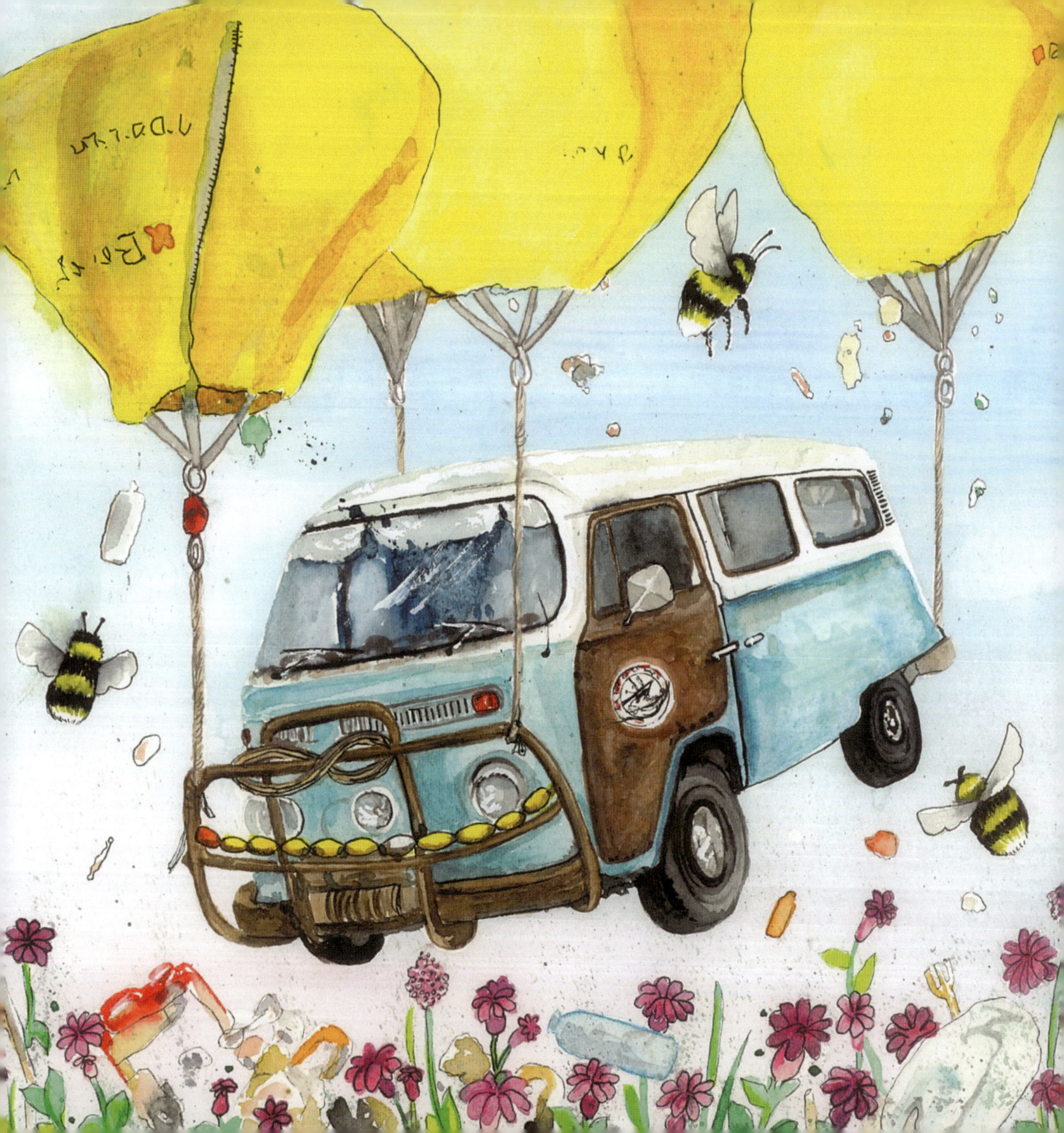

now is old

There were times without clocks
seas without boats
young stones gleamed
on fresh shores
licked by salt lap

Beasts big as buildings
that aren't yet built
trundle knee deep
hunger hangs slack on the bright surface
wide wet mouths
trawl for strange fish
in clean water

Cycads with their narrow leaves
lean over reflections
fizzing with life
and creatures crawl
awkward and uncertain
onto the land
past shells
curling in opposite spiral
not yet ground to sand
or pressed to stone
shining in the brighter light
of a vernal sun

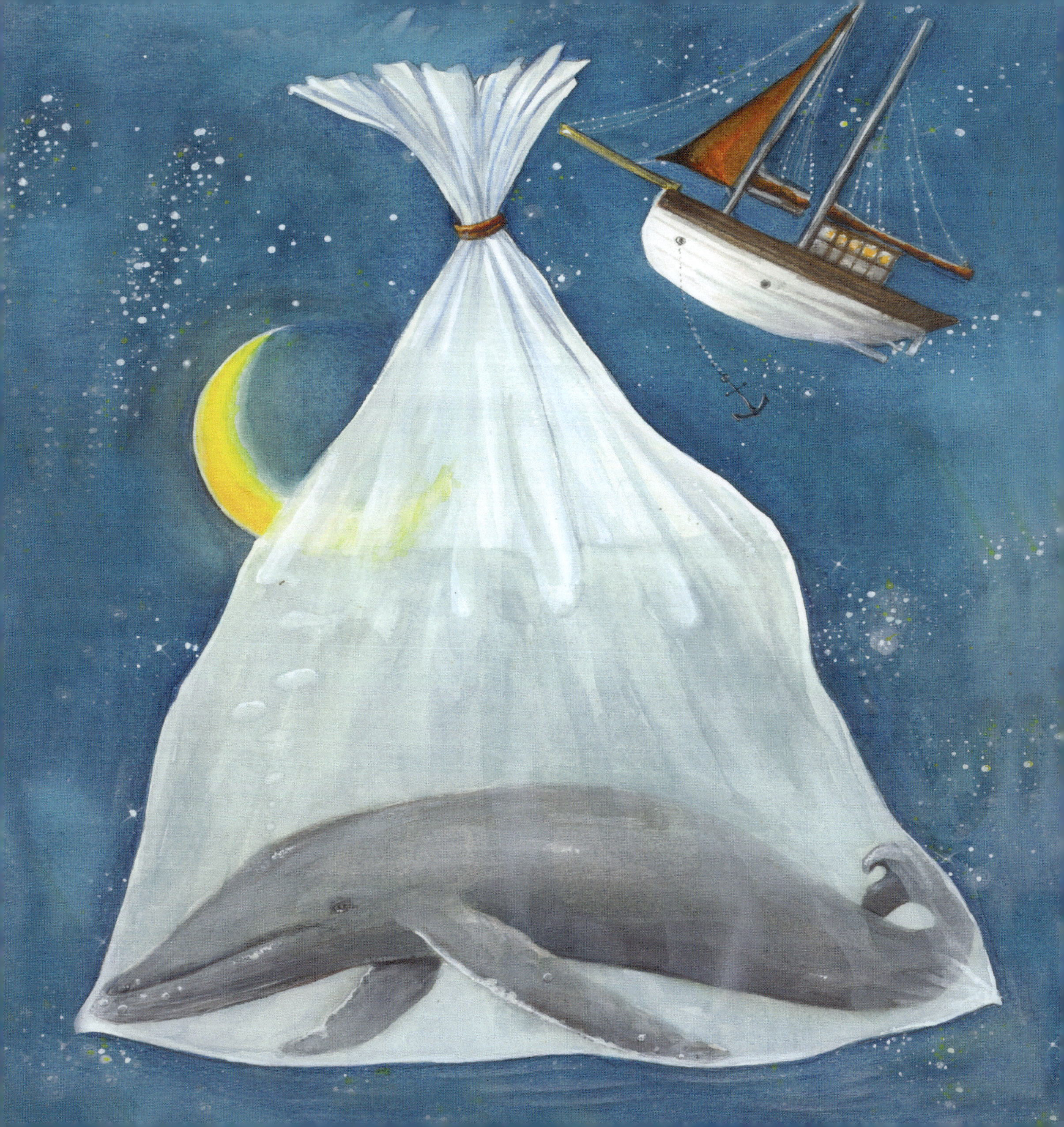

sea sound

when immense waves
rush the cliffs
pale effervescence
riding their wide translucent core
to beat on the shore like a drum
there's a song sings
through the sea
her voice pounding rock
now whispers to sand
then giggles and frolics up and down
hissssss   tick tick tick
a million little gravel clocks
send out their details of time

day and night the moon
tidally locked
looks down at the earth
pulls silver gravity-thread
teases sea   lifts land
          hers is a quiet music
only the quivering water hears
entranced   she takes its whole
colossal body dancing
land looks up
as they shimmy and sway
and all along the shore line
small stones   silt
boulders and soil let go
tumbling into the swell

We are Oceans
babies   75%
me   55%
not passive observers
part of the oneness of water
in an ever changing universe

3 and a half billion years ago
before oxygen clouded the atmosphere
water swam in itself
as we do
aqua molecules aching for release
searching out carbon compounds
seeking to combine and multiply
creating a litany of miracles

Today's seas
sun bathe till their
skin lifts off
rising into the sky
unchecked

We too
fly into finer stuff
given the right conditions
a conducive atmosphere

Release
the earthbound gravity-body
experience the vaults wideness
directly
quietly luminous
cumulonimbus
ready to fall again
into our own
familial ocean

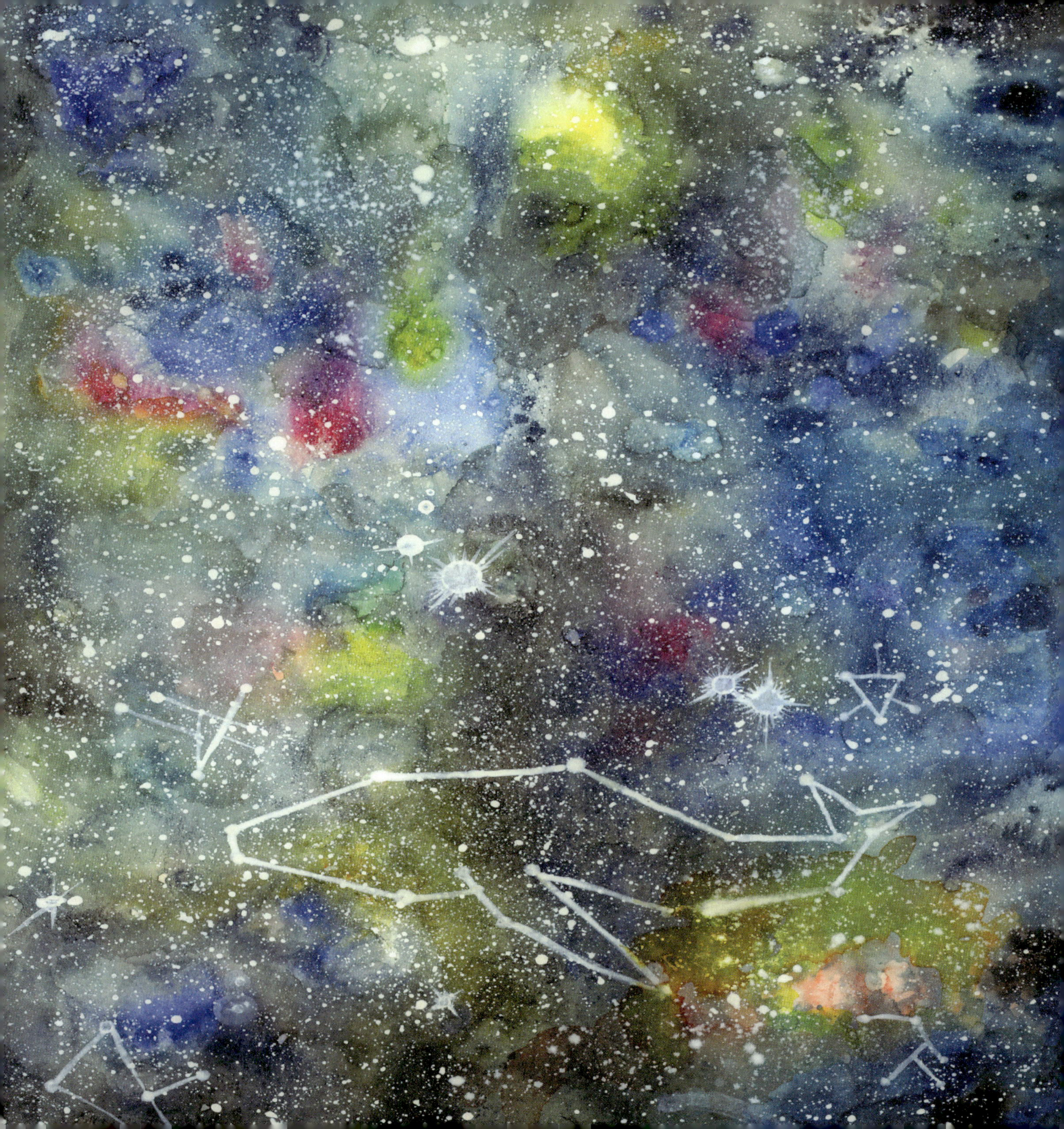

sea and sky

her grey skin
reflects the sky like a mirror
shining in its own way

water has no corners
it collects
then it falls

connecting remoteness
to a sensory projection
of place

woven
molecular alignments
presenting as solid

the eye
stripped naked
sees oceans of debris

plunge your head
into the froth
draw salt

breathe
until your skin
sisters the sky

slip
silently
into the leaded mirror

Milk

Far away
out where it's deep as the sky
near the surface
where light splits water
in gentle tessellations

the pilot whale skin to skin
presses her warm blood body
against a slick new calf
sings her joy
to kin four thousand miles away
around them
close family
spiral in silver fizz

baby pushing back
searches
milk cloud blossoms

after that first feed
                    silence

his small body spinning
into the depths

the blackfish mother
catches him
 cradles in careful fins
keens salt into salt

their family spiral slowly
follow for days
appetite gone
squid swim past

untroubled by their quiet
passage

sir Attenborough said
it could be plastic
curdled her milk
 toxic industrial chemicals
adsorbing micro-particles
caught in the food chain
 krill to cod

we watch her
wondering
how she will ever let go

Oxygen / Food

Imagine the blow hole blocked
air wheezing past plastic

enormous mammals
struggling for breath

stranded like the smoker
unable to climb the stairs

who stands
weeping

as light refracts
and colour rushes away

oxygen loss takes them both
gasping   into the darkness

*

Look up
a dark disc

drifts near the surface
scalloped edges scattering light

casts its bulletproof eyes
into the tide

hunting with its grim
retracted beak

for flouncing radiant jellyfish
throat already filled

with long chains
of ethyl polymers

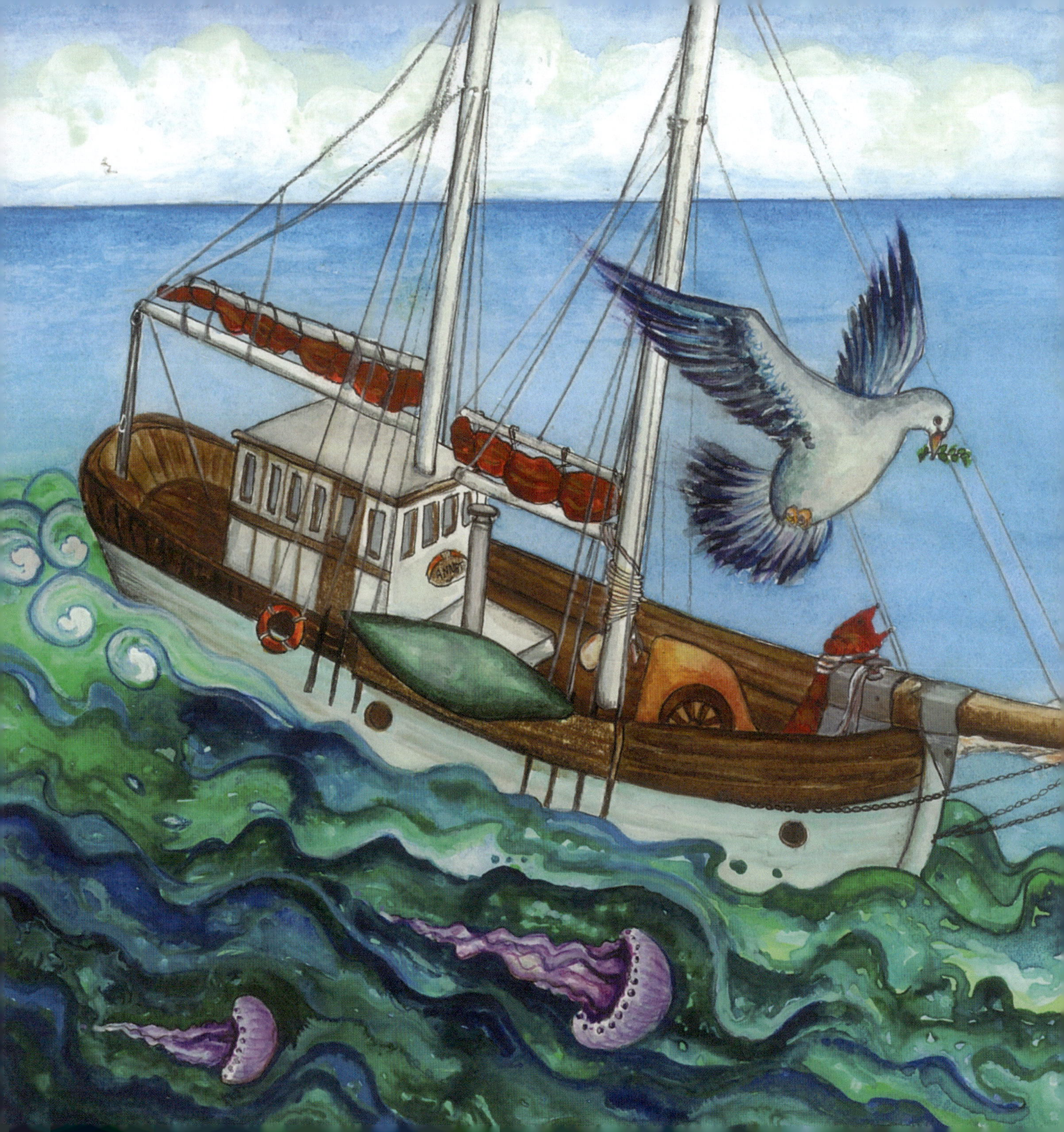

I, Water

Who are these people kneeling in the pebbles
sawing old rope with sharp knives
cutting out loops
and knots   caught fast
in a tumble of rock
Each has a bag big enough to climb in

A zillion kilos
unbelievable lengths lost at sea
THE MOST DURABLE ROPE IN THE WORLD
rendered
to micro-existence
flows into us and everything

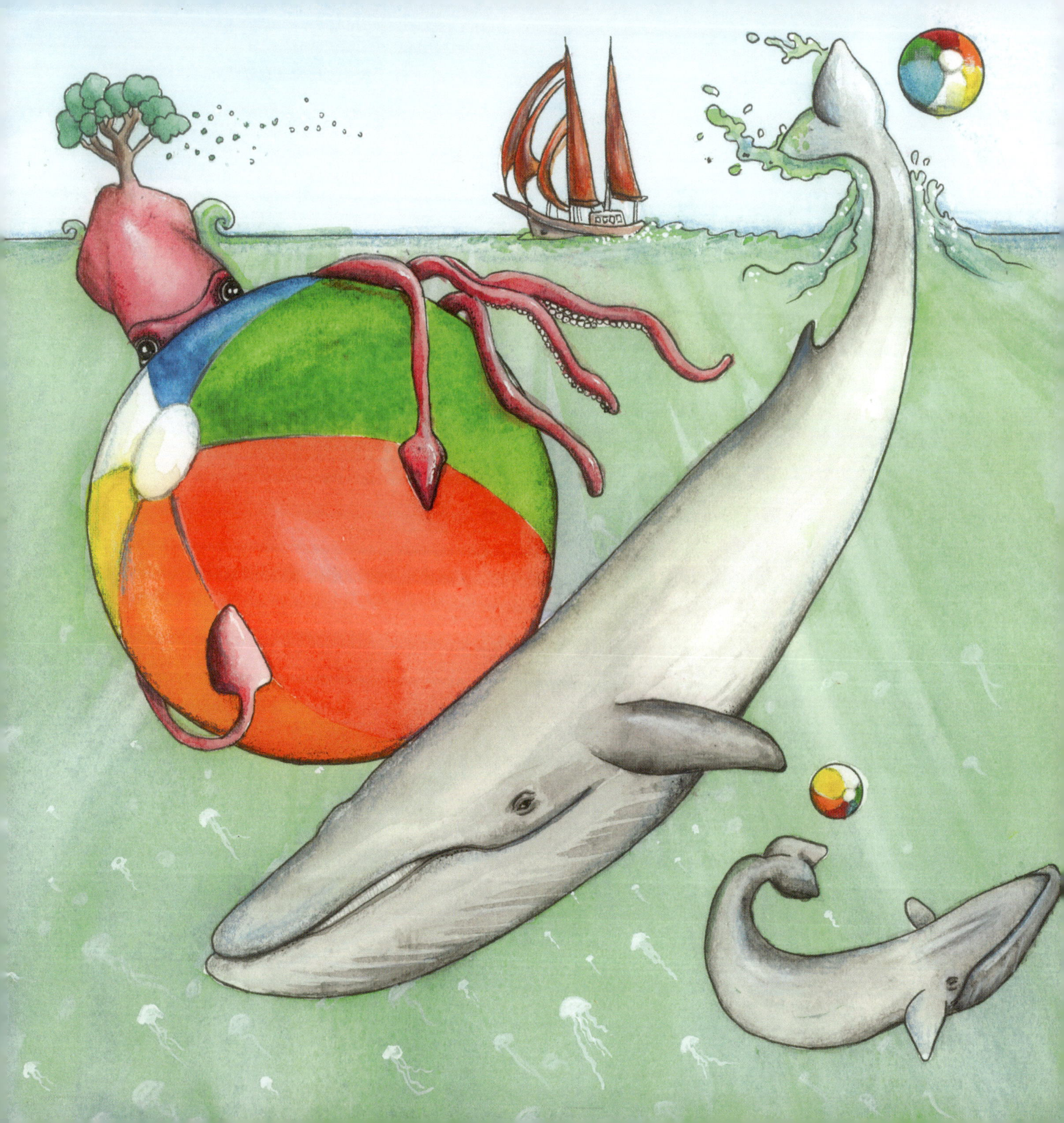

Saline

Coppiced shoreline
black   brine soaked roots
rock teeth snarling with detritus

sea-slap
spits and draws gobfulls
micro-shining from a luminous halo
of scumbling grey froth

tugs bright tendrils of rope
reaching with thin yearning
from beneath the weight
of dark stones

Day 1
14th Feb 2020
Between a Shout and a Son

we manage the surface
the washed wounds of entanglement

contrast pressure-hosed marine creatures
with pulverized grains
-jaunty bottles
-anthropogenic debris

tape bandages to the surface

she was all belly   head stranded
eyes filled
     with plastic

10 days   10 beaches
find an old paddl
bring whale-water in plastic bags

with each breath
she balloons
     slowly

unwrap the bottle
pour in turn
empty it carefully over her eyes

she was enormous
                singing with halitosis
a petroleum sourced yacht
                scudded along her body

water ponds
around her
blood
the size of elephants
breathing into the knowledge gap

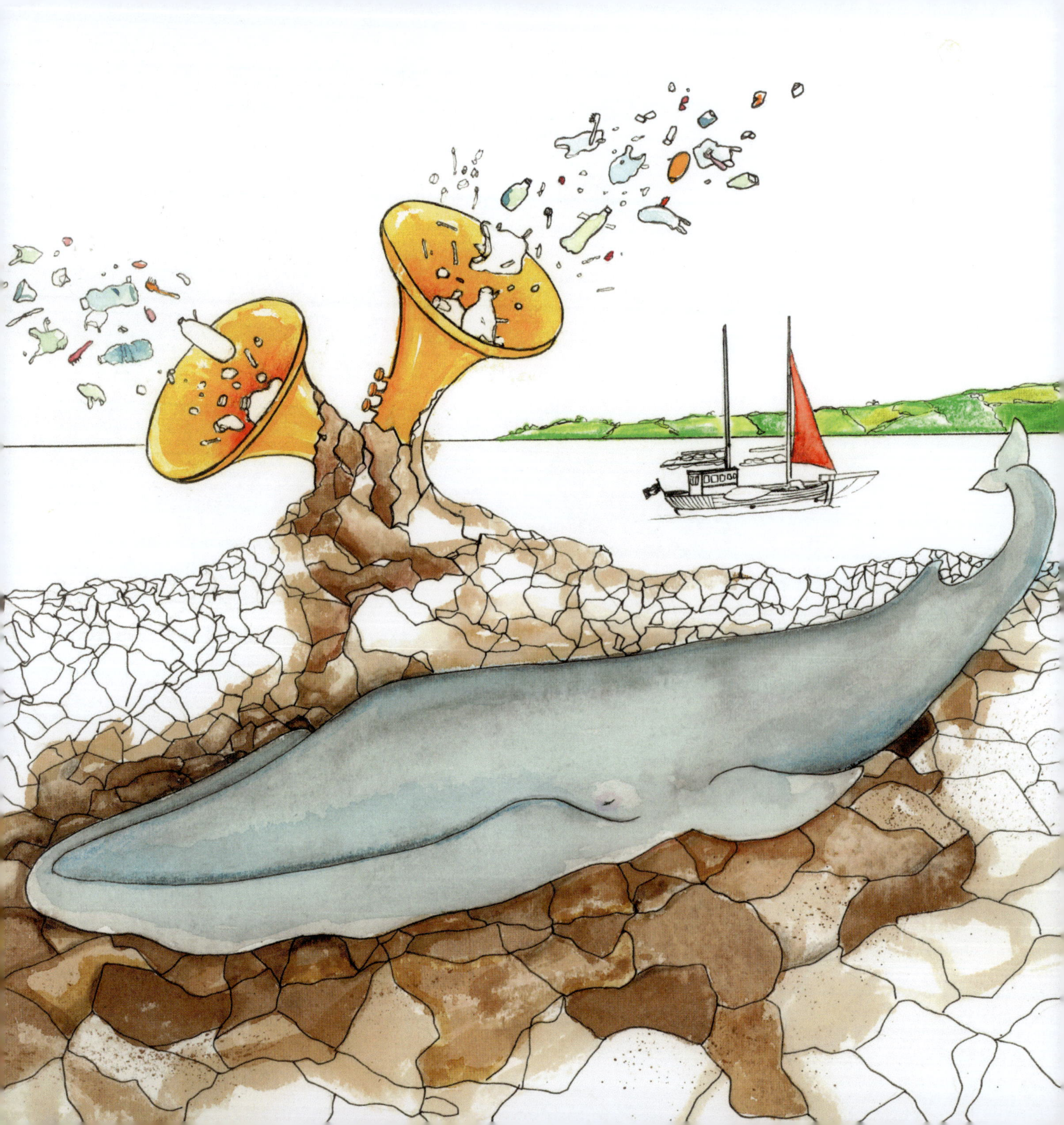

atmospheric chaos

There's sand in the storm
our stinging eyes bleed
in a bleakness of salt
great bubbly breakers
churn
line   rope   sail and net
A film noir hintingly cynical
searching for culprits
deep in the world's water
Why this plastic attitude
can't we legislate
demonstrate
stand on the shore of the storm
compassionately
preen and groom this body of water
settle her heaving anxiety

Annie

In the wood of the boat is a song
her timber tells stories
keens to the sea
is a skin
is a cupped hand
is a home

She listens for the slip slap
her flock
shoal
dark sharky kayaks
hauling home old rope
odds
ends
nets   floats   a broken Openel

She holds it all
suffers the kilos
settles more deeply
her surfaces describe boundaries
Under the waterline her people sleep

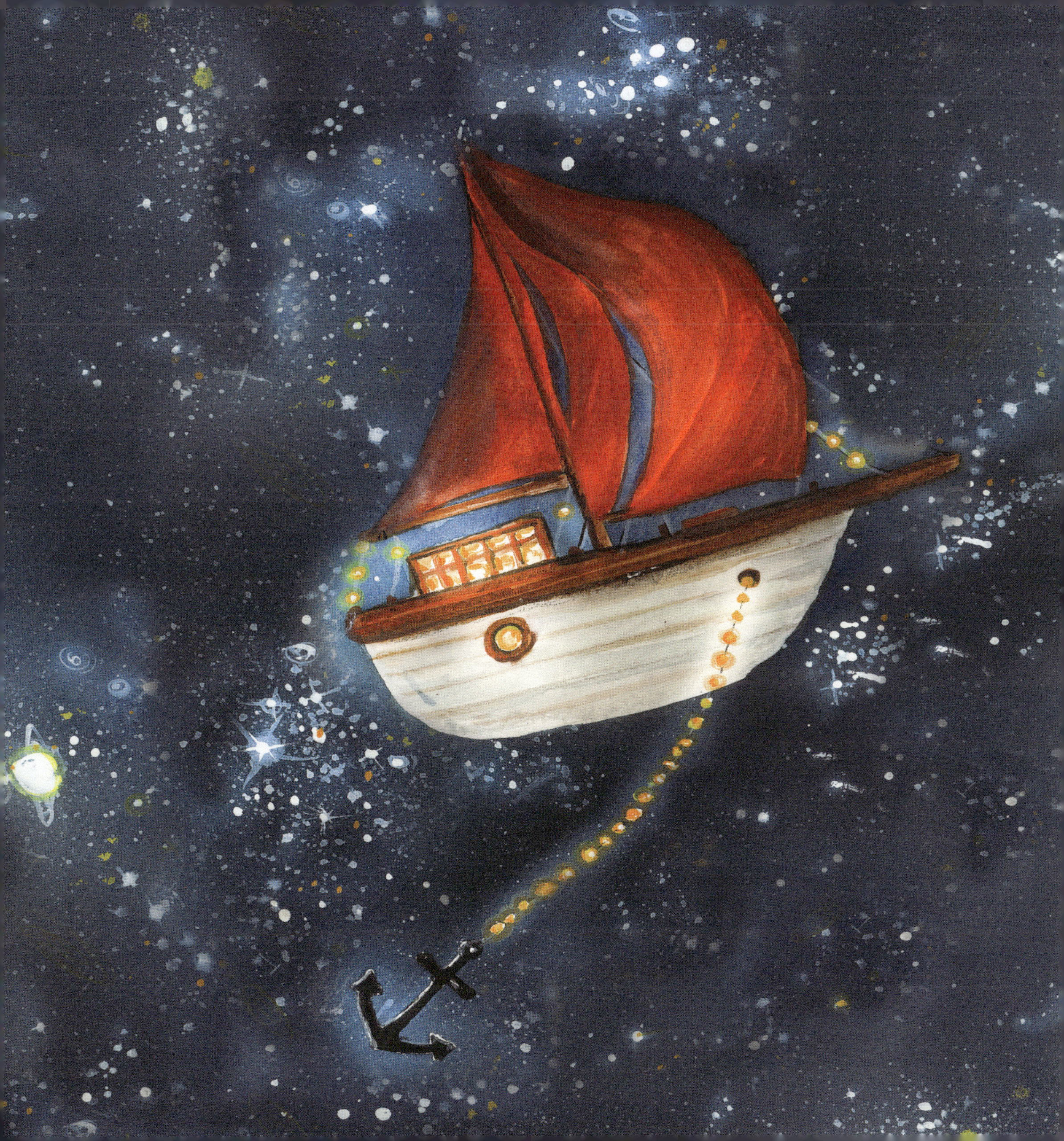

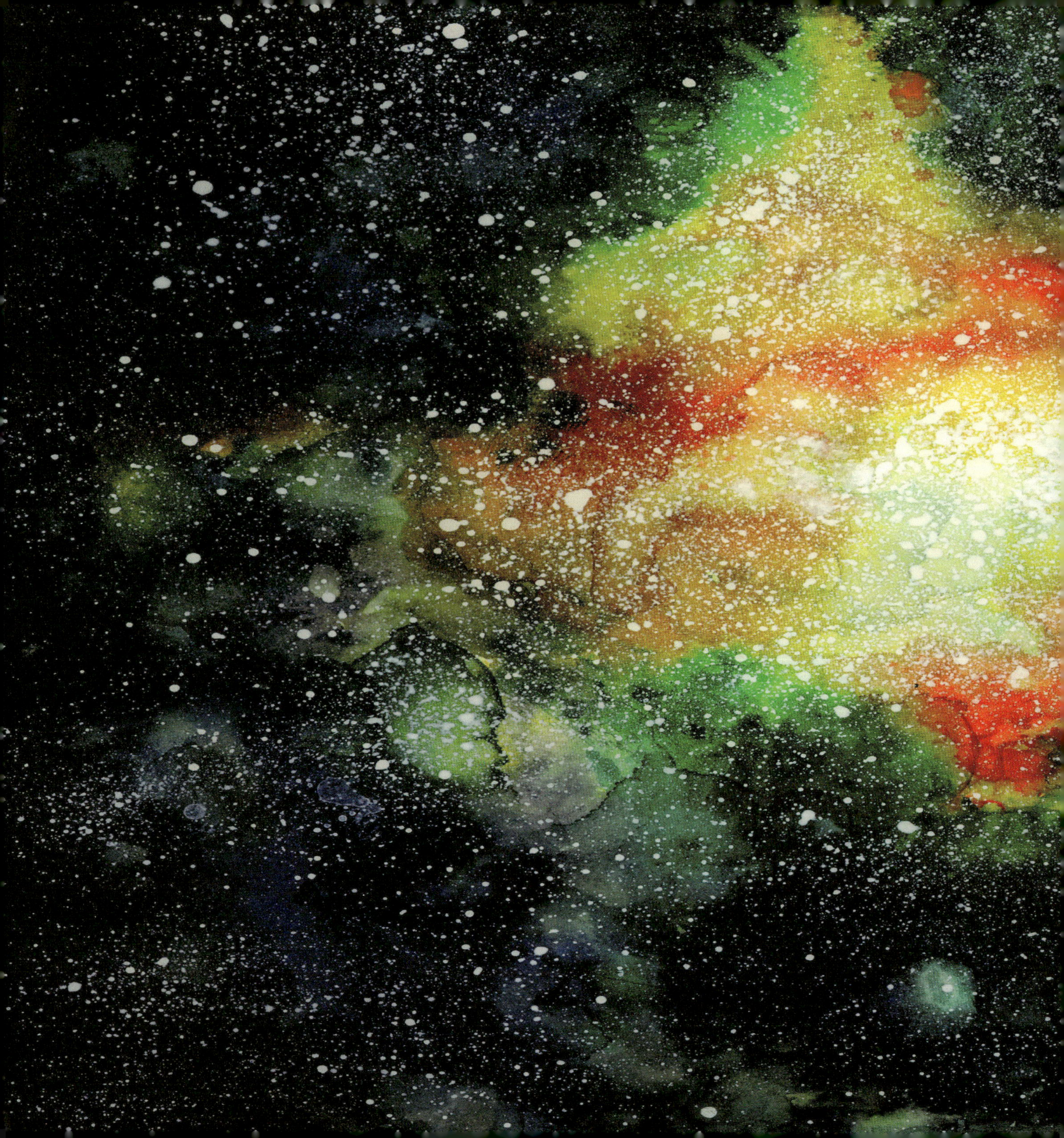

Day 9
25th February 2020

We identified items
balloons   abandoned mechanisms
an old boat   rope
Returned to the world
collecting its tiny mirrors
fishing for Aphrodite
Our little glass and metal dory
creates the thinnest legend
More than sea fragments
bursting
full of impact sparkle
As if we breathe rain
bits of tyre harnessing sunlight
The most beautiful woman
a bloom of plastic bags
visible from space
We in this world full of stars
collect rubbish
Strong arms
Strands of hair
Smell of sea plastic

Murmuration of Sea Plastic

Shoal of blues
distance murmurating bright fragments

light journey's into the deep
on small surfaces
glittering like stars
           starlings

as if night broke in a billion pieces
and threw itself
           fast as a large net emptying
back in the ocean
the colours fall
into water and light

caught in a quickness of current
they move together
turning like birds

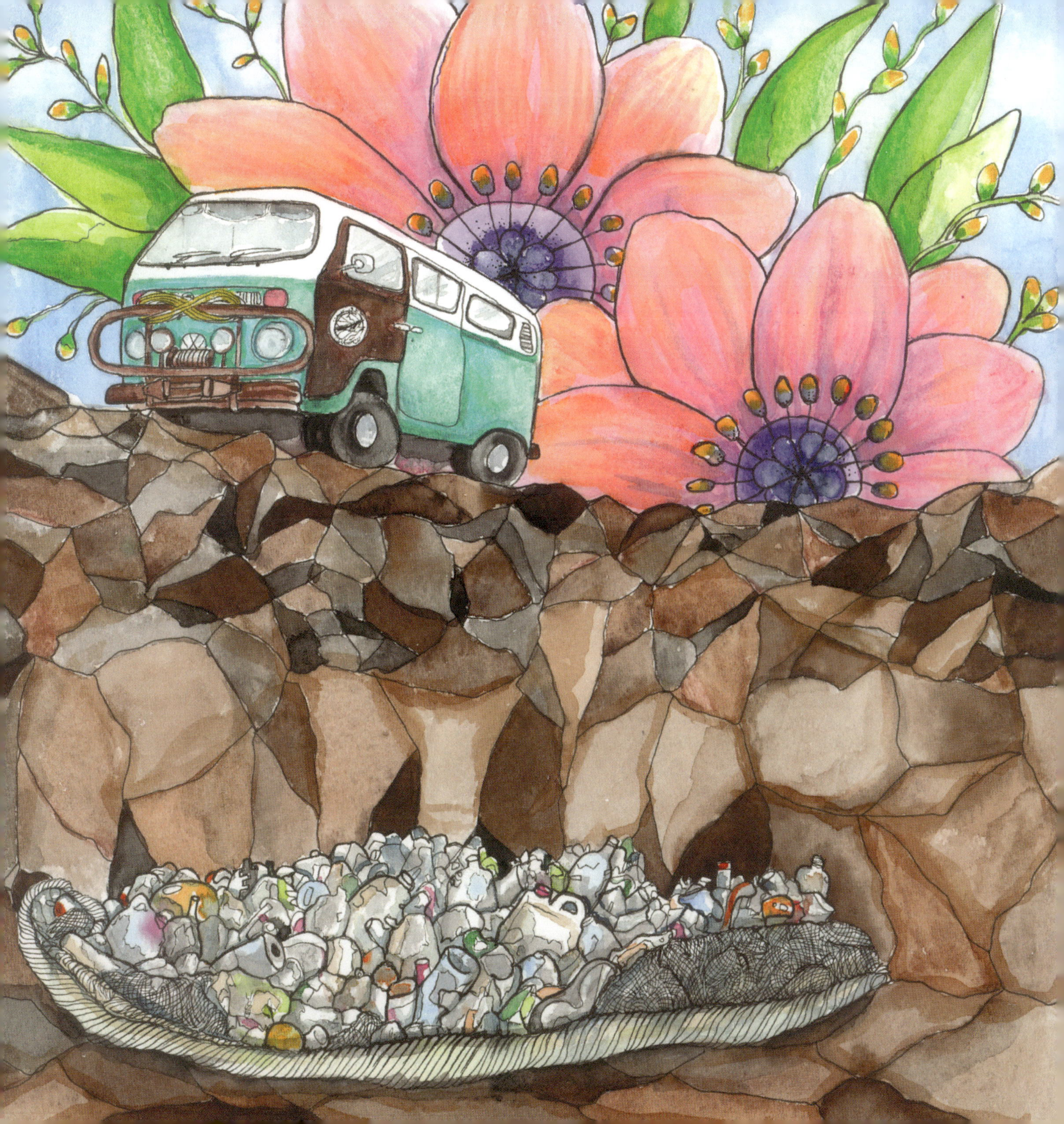

clear

all this abuse
and still clear

it is her nature

sustaining
creating

a sea of beingness

now silver green
now gold and grey

nothing out there
can fathom her

Summer of Saws

Steve mends the boat with bare hands
knuckles down
bending timbers twice his size

a roasting sun lays tree shadow
in stripes
on the shiny mud

bordering his beached boat
displaying it's inner world
through the breach in her hull

a summer of saws
he hammers in ginger haze
quiet   confident

their snuffly old
sea dog
smells the wind

and his family watch
gazing out through the hole
hoping it doesn't rain

Entering Exmouth

The Annette's bow
sends rising surf
streaming down the carvel oak
of mended hull
she enters through the narrow gate
that guides us on a deeper path

There's the gap
to starboard
sucking the boisterous waves
between sandbank and raggy rock
a black seawall
gussied with barnacles
streams of weed
gleaming in six o'clock sun

To port water boils and leaps
in frenzy over submerged sands
We hug the sharper shore
believe in fourteen meter depth
come in with the tide
swept round the corner
into a wide estuary
rimmed by boats

Waves flatten

gutter a million golden eyes
winking
as we look for green lights
set careful course
keep keel from sand
moved around
by heavy storm
and rushing tide

We creep past paddle boarder
bobbing taxi's
waving at each other as they pass
fetching and carrying
their evening traffic
wind surfer   water skier
evening fisher   work over
a matching shoal of little boats
a school of sails

Fishermen
who power past
with sailors caps and steady gaze
serious with ready nets
bloom of green on metal frame
a string of orange plastic buoys
along the back

Across the creek
a tiny train
describes a line along the edge
yellow windows form a chain
that slowly moves
through shadows
on the darkening shore

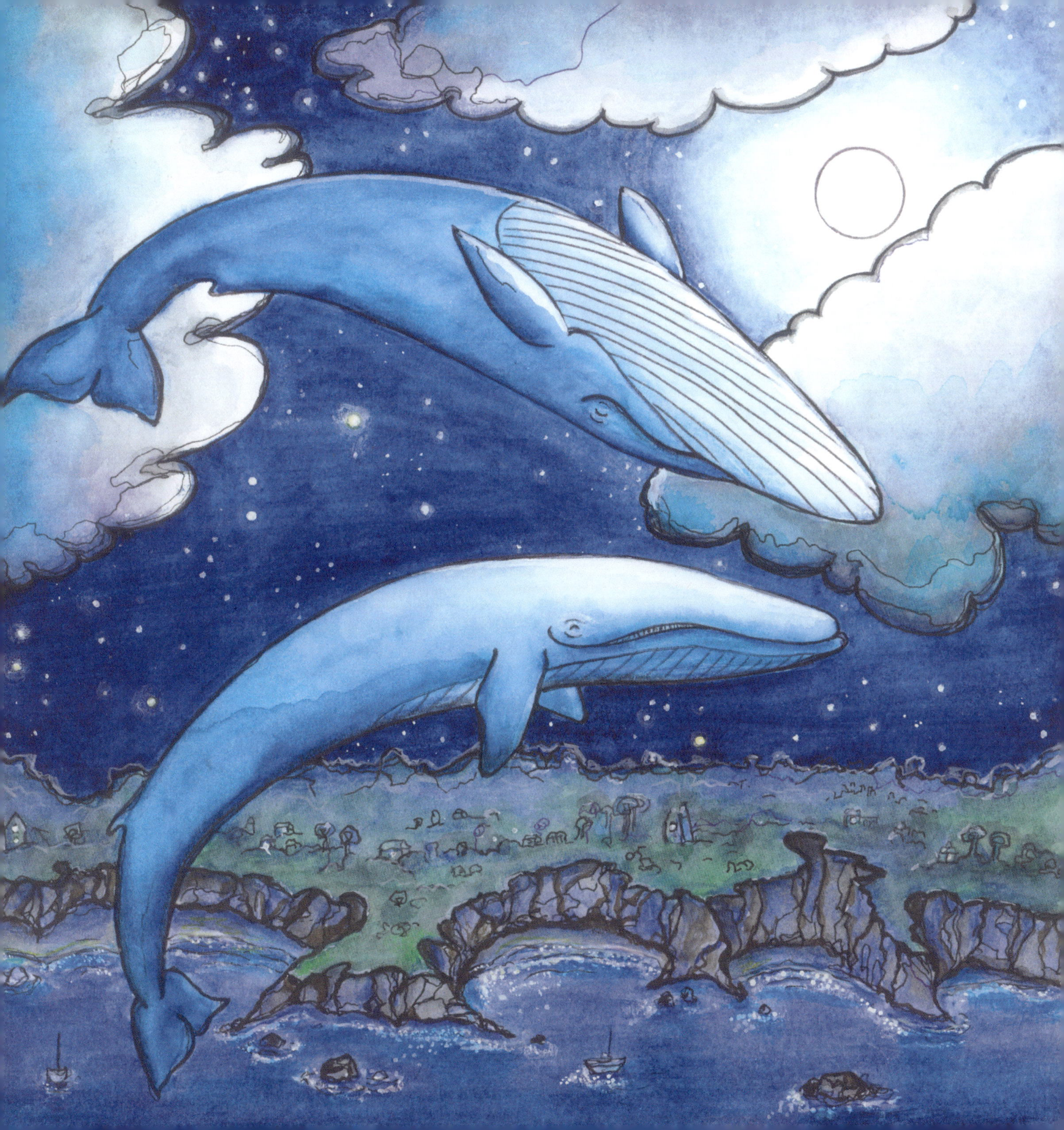

Ghost Gear

pacific antarctic atlantic indian
shades of blue
map impossible borders

global fishermen
fill the ocean that feeds them
trade ghost gear
for throw back

trawlers trail nets
could catch carparks
cathederals
fish in their trillions
a great white whale

no witnesses

just 100,000
fishermen
earning their living
      enslaved
slitting our scaly sisters
in factories
letting loose their buoys
losing a billion bits of rope
and gloves

shhhhh
cast not
this net across the sea

Turf Lock

beside the green
people reef
the schooner's sails
fore and aft
leech and luff
her gaff rig stashed
too long
to navigate the lock
she stops in river water
silky mud trails
stream out along the tide
taking the last light
deep beneath the surface
as they dock

   *

Morning wears a cold mist
curious eidolons
become a cluster of kayaks
row boats knock their arrival
on Annie's hull
hands pass plastic
polypropylene   ethylene
pet
weighed and sorted
into massive bags and nets
down onto tottering hulls

red yellow green blue
pink and purple mountains
paddled slowly
dwarfing the puny humans
wobbling into Exeter's
shipping canal
stopping often to rest
they lean their damp hair on surfaces
bright as the day they were made

both banks are reachable
framing
this strange caravan
convoy
cumulation
this everything we ever thought to gain
come back to haunt us
this rubbish barge
       making its slow way
back to the city

    *

Here are hands
reaching down
lifting the weighed weight
of plastics
onto the bank
the council
ready to start recycling
turning the whole damn lot
into black kayaks

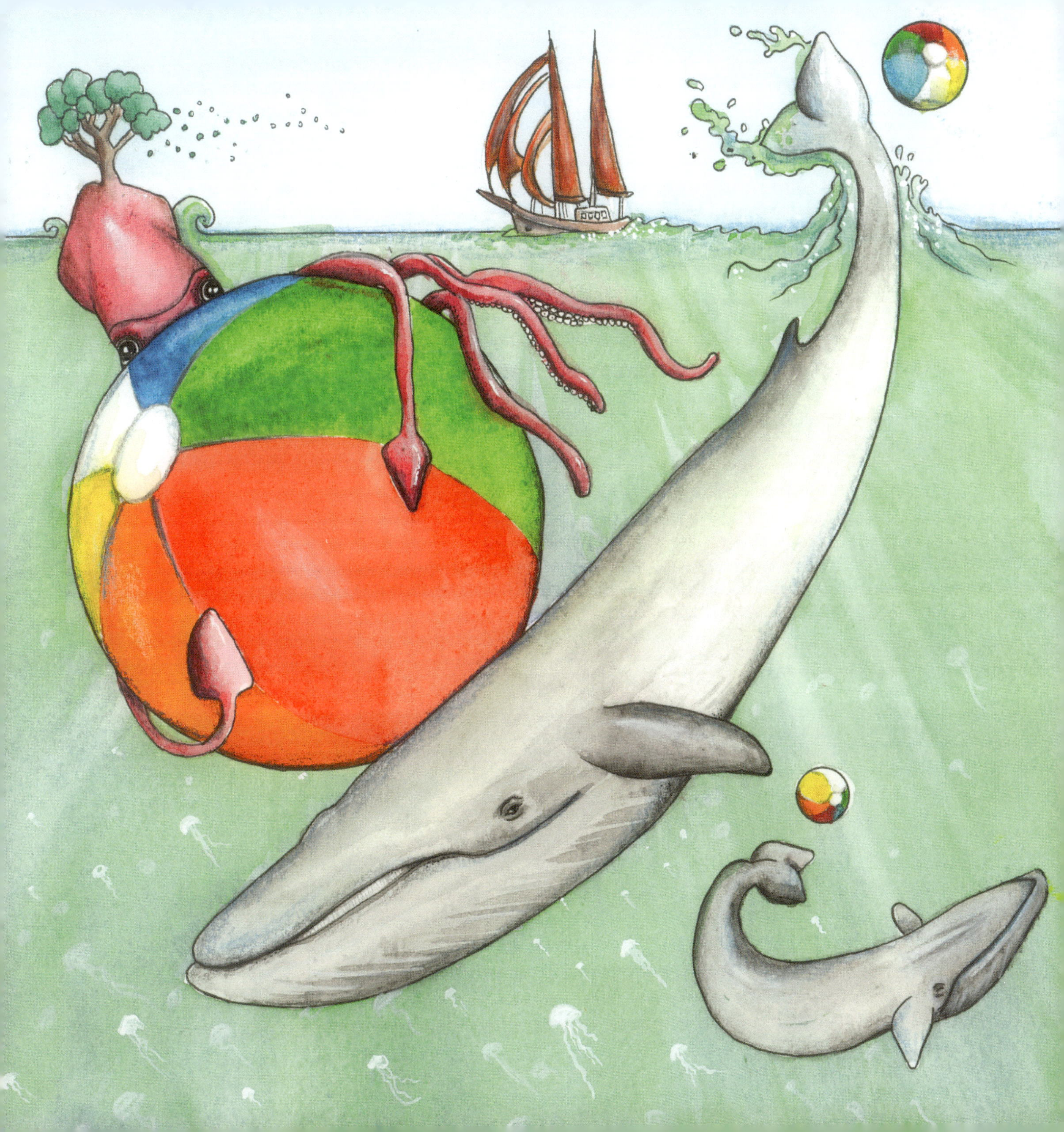

We are on a mission to remove marine pollution from the hard to reach parts of our shores.

We founded Clean Ocean Sailing with the aim of cleaning our coasts and oceans sustainably under sail, and raising awareness about ocean plastics. We are restoring our 115-year old sailing boat The Annette - mothership of Clean Ocean Sailing.

We are
- Sailing, rowing and paddling to inaccessible places to collect marine litter
- Running workshops on repurposing and recycling marine litter
- Raising awareness in our community about the amount of plastic waste in our marine environment and the damage it does
- Inspiring a wider audience to join the fight against plastic pollution by organising shared events and experiences
- Restoring 'The Annette' as a craft with an environmental mission

We have owned our beloved boat The Annette for just over 15 years now. She is a gaff-rigged schooner, 66 foot, 55 tonnes, extremely strong carvel oak planked on oak frames. She was built to sail in the harshest conditions and is, to this day, extremely seaworthy.

For her 110th birthday we are giving her a vital new purpose. She is going fishing again, but this time not for fish - for marine plastic!

We started weighing, counting and recording the amount of marine litter that we collected on our cleanups in December 2017. Since then, we have collected over 55 tons of man-made rubbish from the sea.

More than 200 volunteers have joined us, lending a hand in their various areas of expertise to help us make the movement work in bigger scale. They help us on cleanups, in restoring The Annette, with social media, office work, graphic design, making videos, writing articles, talking to and helping businesses to become plastic free, coordinating events and motivating us to continue to carry on with our vital mission.

We are very grateful and happy to have this amazing team of volunteers on board with us at Clean Ocean Sailing. We wouldn't be able to achieve any of this without volunteers, partners and our financial supporters!

Let's create a bigger community to continue looking after our marine environment on a wider scale. The ocean is huge, and we are just tiny fish swimming in it. We are committed to doing our best to clean up the horrendous amount of plastic litter that humans are putting in to the rivers and ocean each moment, and we'd love to have you on board.

You can be part of Clean Ocean Sailing right now.

Become our Patron.

For more details visit www.cleanoceansailing.com or follow us on social media.

Best wishes,

Steve and Monica

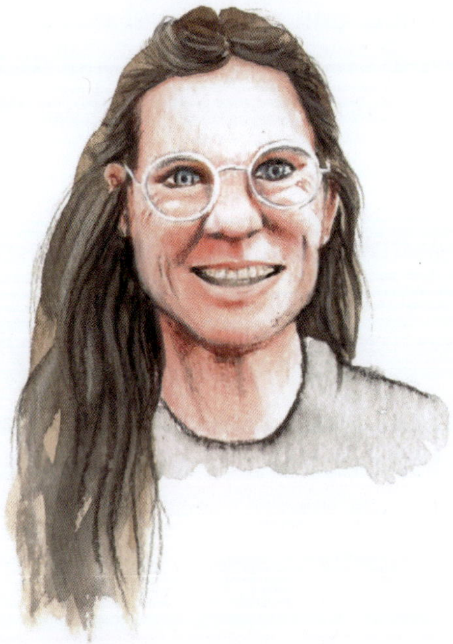

This book is a touching tribute to the late Morag Smith, who co-authored it but passed away close to its publication on July 26, 2023. Morag had a gift for poetry, and her loss is deeply felt by those who knew her, and by those who would have discovered her through her work.

Although she is no longer with us, Morag has left behind a substantial body of work, some of which has already been published, and more will be released after her passing.

Morag was a dedicated advocate for the underprivileged and the environment, and her Buddhist beliefs highlighted the importance of personal transformation leading to global change.

She was an extraordinary example of strength, vitality, wisdom, and compassion. May her poetry and words serve as inspiration for all of us to take action and contribute to making the world a better place, starting with ourselves.

My dear and beautiful friend. It brings both a sense of sorrow and gratitude to reflect upon the journey we've shared. Having the privilege of your friendship and the opportunity to collaborate with you has been an immense pleasure that words can hardly capture.

As we bid farewell to your earthly presence, I take solace in the thought that your spirit now soars in the boundless realm of the heavens. Your laughter echoes in the gentle breeze, your wisdom resonates in the rustling leaves, and your kindness lives on in the hearts of all those you touched.

May your journey beyond be as radiant and serene until we meet again, dear friend, may you find peace in the embrace of the heavens.

Printed in Great Britain
by Amazon